DATE DUE

FRANCE
the people

Greg Nickles

A Bobbie Kalman Book

The Lands, Peoples, and Cultures Series

 Crabtree Publishing Company

The Lands, Peoples, and Cultures Series

Created by Bobbie Kalman

Coordinating editor
Ellen Rodger

Project development, editing, and design
First Folio Resource Group, Inc.
  Pauline Beggs
  Colin Christie
  Tom Dart
  Kathryn Lane
  Alana Perez
  Debbie Smith

Separations and film
Embassy Graphics

Printer
Worzalla Publishing Company

Consultants
Thérèse Sabaryn, University of Waterloo;
Daphnée Saurel

Photographs
Archive/Photo Researchers: p. 9 (left); Van Bucher/Photo Researchers: p. 17 (top); Catherine Cabrol/Explorer/Photo Researchers: title page; Mark Cator/Impact: p. 11 (left); Corbis/Jonathan Blair: p. 4; Corbis/Michael Boys: p. 26 (bottom); Corbis/Ales Fevzer: p. 20 (top); Corbis/Owen Franken: cover, p. 11 (top right), p. 18 (right), p. 22 (left), p. 23 (top), p. 27 (bottom), p. 30 (right), p. 31 (bottom); Corbis/Annie Griffiths Belt: p. 25; Corbis/Stephanie Maze: p. 15 (top and bottom), p. 18 (left); Corbis/Jim Sugar Photography: p. 22 (right); Corbis/Peter Turnley: p. 29 (bottom); Corbis/Adam Woolfitt: p. 27 (top); Peter Crabtree: title page, p. 5 (bottom left), p. 7 (bottom side), p. 10, (bottom) p. 13 (top left and bottom), p. 16 (top, middle, bottom), p. 23 (bottom), p. 26 (top), p. 29 (top, middle); Doisneau/Rapho/Photo Researchers: p. 9 (right); Herve Donnezan/Photo Researchers: p. 17 (bottom); Gregory Edwards/International Stock Photo: p. 14; David R. Frazier/Photo Researchers: p. 28 (top); Gaillard/Jerrican/Photo Researchers: p. 5 (top right); Giraudon/Art Resource, NY: p. 6; Richard Hackett/International Stock Photo: p. 11 (bottom right); George Haling/Photo Researchers: p. 27 (middle), p. 28 (bottom); Bobbie Kalman: p. 5 (top left); Alain Le Garsmeur/Impact: contents page; Erich Lessing/Art Resource, NY: p. 8; Bruno Maso/Photo Researchers: p. 31 (top); Alain Nicolas/Explorer/Photo Researchers: p. 13 (top right); Richard T. Nowitz: p. 24 (bottom); Richard Phelps Frieman/Photo Researchers: p. 30 (left); Reuters/Daniel Joubert/Archive Photos: p. 21; Reuters/Jean Paul Pelissier/Archive Photos: p. 20 (bottom); Stan Ries/International Stock Photo: p. 12; Ray Roberts/Impact: p. 15 (middle); Scala/Art Resource, NY: p. 7 (top); Sabine Weiss/Photo Researchers: p. 24 (top); Ulrike Welsch/Photo Researchers: p. 5 (bottom left)

Illustrations
David Wysotski, Allure Illustrations: back cover

Cover: A man hoists a huge platter of fresh seafood at a restaurant in Paris.

Title page: A Versaille oyster shop owner stands outside his business. The sign says he sells oysters in the shell all year long.

Icon: The *fleur-de-lys* was the emblem of the French kings.

Back cover: Gothic cathedrals such as Notre Dame are decorated with grotesque ornamental figures called gargoyles.

Published by
Crabtree Publishing Company

PMB 16A
350 Fifth Avenue
Suite 3308
New York
N.Y. 10118

612 Welland Avenue
St. Catharines
Ontario, Canada
L2M 5V6

73 Lime Walk
Headington
Oxford OX3 7AD
United Kingdom

Cataloging in Publication Data
Nickles, Greg, 1969-
    France --the people / Greg Nickles.
    p.cm. -- (Lands, peoples, and cultures series)
    "A Bobbie Kalman book"
    Includes index.
    Summary: Text and photographs present the history and accomplishments of the people of France.
    ISBN 0-86505-322-7 (paper) -- ISBN 0-86505-242-5 (rlb.)
    1. France--Social conditions--Juvenile literature. 2. France-- Social life and customs--Juvenile literature. I. Title. II. Series.
    HN425.5.N52 2000
    j944   LC00-026066
                  CIP

Contents

 Love of life

The rich history of the French people is filled with famous rulers, powerful **empires**, and great accomplishments. The French, who are deeply attached to their country and traditions, are known for their *joie de vivre*, or love of life. They enjoy eating fine foods, shopping for fashionable clothes, playing all kinds of sports, and celebrating special days with family and friends.

Liberty, equality, and brotherhood

Throughout the centuries, the powerful ideas of great French thinkers influenced people around the world. In the 1700s, French **philosophers** proposed the ideas of *liberté, égalité,* and *fraternité,* or freedom, equality, and brotherhood.

These ideas suggested that all people are members of one large family. They should be treated as equals and have certain basic rights that their rulers should never be able to take away. Many modern **democracies** are founded on these important concepts.

The French are also known as leaders in world politics. France was a founding member of the United Nations, whose mission is to protect human rights around the world, and the European Union, a trade organization in Western Europe.

(top) Basque shepherds shear sheep in the Pyrénées Mountains, in southwest France.

(above) A boy carries home a loaf of freshly baked bread.

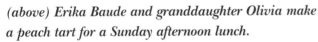

(above) Erika Baude and granddaughter Olivia make a peach tart for a Sunday afternoon lunch.

(right) A rock climber carefully makes her way up a cliff in the Alps, in southeastern France.

(below) Women pass a local butcher shop and delicatessen after an afternoon of shopping.

Centuries of France

The first known people to live in France were the ancient Celts, who arrived from central Europe in about 1000 B.C. In 52 B.C., soldiers from the Roman Empire in Italy **conquered** the Celts. The Romans ruled the region, which they called Gaul, for over 500 years. They introduced their culture and language to the Celts, and built many cities throughout the country.

Vercingetorix was the leader of the last Gauls to hold out against the Romans. This painting, from 1899, shows his surrender to Julius Caesar, the ruler of Rome, in 52 B.C.

Early France

In 486 A.D., a people called the Franks **invaded** from the northeast and took over Gaul. The area they invaded became known as France, after the new rulers. The Franks' leaders, including the powerful Charlemagne, controlled the country for centuries. They faced many challenges to their rule. When they were not quarreling among themselves, the rulers fought off attacks by other peoples such as the Normans. The Normans were Vikings from Scandinavia. They eventually took over an area on France's northern coast that is now called Normandy. In 1066, they also conquered England.

Charlemagne is crowned emperor on December 25, 800.

Joan of Arc

After the English king tried to **claim** the French throne, the two countries fought a series of battles that lasted from 1337 to 1453. This period became known as the Hundred Years' War. By 1429, France had lost much of its territory to England. Then, a young French **shepherdess** named Joan of Arc appeared before her country's leaders. She said that voices from heaven told her that she would bring victory to France. The leaders were convinced of Joan of Arc's power. They let her command a battle at Orléans, a city in northwest France which was long-surrounded by English **troops**. Riding on horseback and dressed in armor, she inspired her soldiers to save the city. This stunning triumph gave the French new confidence to win the war.

Joan was captured soon after her victory, and the English accused her of witchcraft. Found guilty, she was burned at the **stake** in 1431. Joan was only nineteen years old when she died. A French hero, Joan was recognized in 1920 as a saint, or holy person, by the Roman Catholic Church.

This statue of Joan of Arc (right) stands in Paris's Place des Pyramides, near the spot she was wounded fighting the English in 1429.

The French Revolution

Problems continued through most of the 1700s. By the 1780s, the government of King Louis XVI was nearly **bankrupt**, and the people were starving. Conditions grew so bad that, on July 14, 1789, a mob stormed Paris's Bastille prison in protest. This event marked the beginning of the French **Revolution**. After the people forced the king to step down, many hoped to build a new **republic**. This republic would have an elected government that was based on the ideas of equality and justice. Instead, years of violence followed, during which the king and thousands of other people died or were **executed**.

Napoleon and beyond

In 1799, a brilliant young general named Napoleon Bonaparte seized control of France. He built a new, stable government with fairer laws and was awarded the title of **emperor**. The ambitious Napoleon led France into many wars and conquered much of Europe. He was finally defeated by the English in 1815, and was sent to St. Helena, an island in the South Atlantic Ocean, where he died the same year. Years of troubles followed, as France was led by other kings and suffered through more revolutions. Finally, in 1871, the French established a new republic. The country prospered as it built new **industries** and claimed many new colonies in Africa and Asia.

The Grand Siècle and Louis XIV

After winning the Hundred Years' War, France's power continued to grow. French explorers traveled the world and claimed distant lands for their country. These lands became France's **colonies**, part of the vast French Empire.

The years from 1600 to 1700 were France's *Grand Siècle,* or "Great Century." During this time, France was home to great philosophers, writers, **architects**, and artists. Louis XIV, who ruled from 1643 to 1715, was the most powerful king in the country's history. During his long **reign**, France won many battles, but it lost others and was forced to give up some of its colonies.

(above) Known as the Sun King, Louis XIV considered himself the light and power of all of France.

Napoleon Bonaparte's horse rears up as it crosses Mont Saint Bernard, in this 1810 painting by Jacques-Louis David.

Modern challenges

France has faced many challenges since World War II. In the 1950s and 1960s, people born in France's Asian and African colonies wanted to form independent countries. **Rebels** in Vietnam and Algeria fought long wars against French soldiers before the French government finally decided to leave.

France experienced more problems in 1968, when millions of French students and workers protested against the government. They were demanding an improved education system as well as better wages and working conditions throughout the country. Eventually, the French government agreed to the protestors' demands. These challenges have helped France grow into a strong and wealthy country, with modern industries and an exciting culture.

The World Wars

In the first half of the twentieth century, France became a bloody battleground for two devastating wars. In both World War I (1914–18) and World War II (1939–45), Germany invaded the country. While Germany did not succeed in taking over France during World War I, it **occupied** the country during World War II. The French fought back under the leadership of General Charles de Gaulle. In 1944, with the help of the **Allies**, the French won back control of their land. In 1958, de Gaulle became president of France. It took decades for France to recover from the wartime destruction and the deaths of millions of its people.

General Charles de Gaulle leads a procession down Les Champs Élysées to mark the liberation of Paris on August 25, 1944.

The French are **descendants** of many peoples, including the Celts, Romans, Franks, and Normans. Each group settled in a different part of the country and developed its own **customs**, traditions, and languages. France is also home to millions of **immigrants** and their families, who brought the customs of their **homeland** to their new country.

The Basques

The Basques live in the Pyrénées Mountains, which stretch across southwest France and northeast Spain. It is believed that the Basques have lived in this area for over 5000 years. No one knows where they came from, and their language, called Euskera, is unlike any other on the European continent. Today, many Basques still fish, farm, and herd **livestock** like their ancestors did.

Children play in a park during a school outing near Roman ruins in Nice, which is in southern France.

The Basques are one of the most independent peoples in France. For centuries, they governed their lands, which were gradually taken over by France and Spain. Now, there is a strong Basque movement to make these lands their own again.

The Bretons

The Bretons live in Brittany, a rocky corner of northwest France. This area was first inhabited by ancient Celtic tribes, the **ancestors** of today's Bretons. For centuries, Brittany was an independent kingdom. The people practiced their own customs, spoke the Breton language, and worked as farmers and fishers. Since Brittany became part of France in the 1500s, its people have adopted the French language and culture; however, they still follow many of the traditional Breton ways as well. They learn the Breton language in school and celebrate Celtic holidays such as the Joining of the Hands Festival, which brings together Celtic peoples from all over the world.

Maghrébins

Today, about four million people in France are immigrants or the descendants of immigrants who came to France in the last century. Some are from countries such as Italy, Portugal, Turkey, and Vietnam. The majority, however, are *Maghrébins*. They come from the Maghreb, a part of northern Africa that includes the former French colonies of Algeria, Morocco, and Tunisia.

A man stops to inspect fine cloth being sold in an open-air Paris market.

This elegantly dressed woman shops in Paris's finest clothing stores.

Jackets, scarves, and sweaters keep these friends warm on a cool fall day.

French cities bustle with businesses, traffic, and pedestrians. They offer many exciting attractions such as art galleries, museums, and concert halls. Most cities have a very old center, which was the original town. Beautiful churches, a city hall, and squares decorated with fountains and statues are reminders of a city's past. Cafés, shops, and restaurants line some streets, while others house markets that sell fresh fruit and vegetables, flowers, clothes, art, and books. Beyond the old center, modern offices, apartment buildings, and houses sprawl across the landscape.

Growing and changing

About three-quarters of France's population lives in cities and large towns. The rest live in the countryside. **Urban** areas have grown rapidly since the end of World War II, when millions of people moved to the cities to find work. Today, Paris is France's largest city. It is also the center of government, business, and the arts. Other important cities include Lyon, Marseille, Lille, Toulouse, and Bordeaux.

City homes

In the oldest parts of cities, most people live in buildings that are just a few stories tall. Many of these buildings were once hotels. Rarely is there an elevator. Instead, a central staircase leads people to their apartments, which have high ceilings, fancy trim around the windows and doors, and other old-fashioned touches. In newer parts of cities, people live in single-family homes that are similar to houses in the United States and Canada.

Imagine what it would be like to live in Paris, in these cylinder-shaped apartment buildings!

It might be difficult for a car to drive down this narrow cobblestone street in Rouen, in northern France.

Getting around

Getting around city streets can be an adventure! Cars, trucks, and buses cause frequent traffic jams, even on wide, tree-lined streets. Some of the oldest streets in city centers are cobbled, or paved with bumpy stones, and are just wide enough for one car. Many streets are completely closed to motor vehicles, so people walk or ride a bike to get around.

A gendarme, a French police officer, directs traffic during a very busy rush hour.

In the suburbs

Large, spacious suburbs lie on the outskirts of most cities. Filled with shopping centers, office buildings, movie theaters, high-rise apartment buildings, and large houses, the suburbs are becoming more and more crowded. Some areas, especially those with housing built by the government for people with low incomes, have become very run-down. In the 1980s and 1990s, thousands of residents in these areas protested, forcing the government to begin much-needed **renovations**.

Customers at this outdoor market shop for everything from vegetables to clothes.

In the countryside

The French have a special term to describe the relaxed pace and peacefulness of country life: *la douceur de vivre*, or "the good life." Most **rural** people farm or work at shops or other small businesses. Many families have lived in the same area for generations, but others have moved to the countryside more recently or bought a second home there to escape the hustle and bustle of the city.

In the village

Most villages in France have cobbled streets and buildings that are hundreds of years old. At the heart of these villages is an old market square, surrounded by a church, outdoor cafés, and a few shops. In the early afternoon, the cafés, shops, and other businesses close for a couple hours so that everyone can enjoy a long lunch or nap.

On the farm

France's countryside is dotted with thousands of small family farms, as well as larger farms run by big companies. On small family farms, children help their parents do chores. They milk cows, feed chickens and pigs, and gather eggs. During the harvest, they also help gather the crops. Farming is difficult work, though, so more and more young people are moving to cities to look for work.

Country homes

Many people in the countryside live in large houses with a garden. Some houses are modern, while others are centuries-old farm homes. They usually have a gray or white exterior, and brown, gray, or green shutters on the windows. They are made of stone, or built from wooden beams, with walls of plaster and brick. These farm houses are often attached to a barn or stable.

Laundry dries outside the window of an apartment building in Arles, in the south of France.

(above) A dairy farmer feeds calves while her child watches.

(right) Older homes in the Dordogne region, in southwestern France, have steep and pointed roofs that quickly drain rainwater.

(bottom) A grandfather kisses his grandson who has come to his farm for a tractor ride.

French families were once very large. Children, their parents, grandparents, uncles, and aunts often shared a home. Today, families usually have only one or two children and extended families rarely live together.

(above) The French are so fond of their pets, especially dogs, that they even take them to restaurants when they go out to eat!

Together on Sundays

Family ties are very strong in France. On most Sunday afternoons, relatives gather at a family member's home or at a restaurant to chat and eat a large meal. They greet one another by shaking hands and kissing one another on each cheek. There is plenty of conversation and laughter during the meal, which can last all afternoon.

Family celebrations

Families also get together for holidays and celebrations such as weddings, birthdays, and name days. A name day is like a second birthday. It is observed by members of the Roman Catholic Church. They honor their saints by devoting a day of the year to each of them. French children who are named after a saint celebrate their name day on that saint's day. For example, children named after Saint Clare have their name day on August 11, while those named after Saint Denis celebrate on October 9.

A wedding party gathers at the Hotel des Invalides in Paris. The groom and his father, as well as the bride's father, are all in the military. The Hotel des Invalides contains the army museum and Napoleon's tomb.

Vacation time

French workers have five weeks of vacation each year. Traditionally, people took most of their vacation in the summer. They closed up their homes at the end of July, then headed out of the cities, jamming the trains and highways. So many people left at the same time that city streets became deserted and businesses in town shut down for August. Today, families with children take a number of short vacations throughout the year, when schools are closed for holidays. France's southern seaside resorts are the busiest holiday destinations. Many families prefer a quieter getaway, however, and go camping, stay at their cottage, hike in the mountains, or swim on the Atlantic coast.

(right) A father and son greet each other in the traditional French way.

(below) Family members pack up the car as they prepare to leave for their summer vacation.

Going to school

Many of the world's greatest thinkers were born in France. The country boasts one of the world's highest literacy rates, which means that nearly everyone can read and write. Most children go to public schools, which are free. Some families pay a fee for their children to attend private schools, which are often run by the Roman Catholic Church.

First schools

The first school that many children go to is *maternelle*, or nursery school. Children as young as two go to *maternelle*, but others do not start classes until they are six.

School days

Students spend long hours studying each day, and they have a lot of homework at night. Most students in France do not go to school on Wednesdays. Instead, children in younger grades play sports or attend clubs such as band and choir. Children in older grades have the afternoon off. To make up for their missed classes, some students go to school on Saturday mornings.

Choosing a path

At the age of eleven, students begin four years of *collège*, which is like junior high school. After *collège*, some students continue their education at a senior high school called a *lycée*. Other students decide to learn a **trade**. They begin working part-time as **apprentices** or attend a **technical school**, called a *lycée technique*.

(above) Students at the Sorbonne, France's oldest university, take notes during class.

(left) On her first-day of pre-school, a young girl clutches her mother's hand, hoping that she does not leave.

Class holidays

One popular school tradition is the class vacation. On these special trips, students and their teacher go for a one-week holiday to the seaside, the countryside, an important city, or a mountain resort. During their holiday, students study arts, crafts, nature, or history while having fun and getting exercise.

(top) High school students in Paris gather outside of their lycée waiting for classes to begin.

(below) Art students in Nice, sketch Roman ruins that were built in 2 B.C.

Passing the "*bac*"

In their last year at *lycée*, students must pass a difficult exam called the *baccalauréat* if they wish to attend university. For two years, they prepare for the test by studying a range of subjects, including math, philosophy, science, physical education, and music. The *bac* is so difficult that about one-third of all students fail. Students who score the highest marks on this and other tests, however, may be selected for the *grandes écoles*. The *grandes écoles* are special schools that train youth to take on key roles in government, business, science, and other important fields.

France's geography and weather make it the perfect place for many different sports. People rock climb and ski in the mountains, swim and sail along the coasts, and fish and hunt in the countryside. Spectator sports are also popular. Millions of people regularly follow soccer games, tennis matches, and other sports events on television and on the radio.

The *Tour de France*

Cycling is a favorite activity in France, both as a hobby and professional sport. Each year, the country hosts the *Tour de France*, the world's most famous bicycle race. This all-male competition first took place in 1903. Since 1984, there has also been a *Tour de France Féminin* for women. Millions of people around the world watch the race on television, and spectators regularly pack the roadsides to cheer on competitors as they ride by.

(below) French cyclist Richard Virenque cheers as he wins the fifteenth stage of the 1995 **Tour de France.**

(above) skier starts a long descent through the peaks of the French Alps.

A Porsche driven by a French driver pulls into the lead just after the start of the 24-hour Le Mans race.

A challenging race

Professionals from all over the world compete in the long, grueling *Tour de France*. The race covers about 4800 kilometers (2975 miles) of France's mountains and countryside, and usually crosses into a neighboring country as well. Most cyclists compete in teams of nine. Team members try to complete each stage of the race in the fastest time, but it is even more important that they help their leader win. Some team members ride beside their leader, handing him water or food so he does not have to stop. Others ride in front of their leader to block the wind. Still others might chase down a competitor and try to tire him out, so that their leader can race ahead.

The end of the line

After about three weeks of hard cycling, competitors reach the final stage of the race. Although the route changes each year, it always ends at the same place. Riders race to the finish line down a Paris street called Les Champs Élysées and under the famous Arc de Triomphe **monument**. The winners of the race become heroes and have the great honor of wearing the *Tour's* yellow cycling shirt.

Car racing

The French also love car racing, a sport that was invented in France. The country's best-known car race is the *Le Mans*. During this event, teams race for 24 hours non-stop, trying to go as far as possible while traveling at dangerous speeds of up to 400 kilometers (250 miles) per hour. The winning team is the one that drives the furthest. Other car races that attract millions of French spectators include the Monaco *Grand Prix* and the Monte Carlo Rally. Both races are hosted by the tiny kingdom of Monaco on the French Riviera, along France's southeast coast.

The ball game

The traditional game of *pétanque* is very popular in France, especially among older people. The object of the game is to toss metal balls, called *boules*, so that they land as close as possible to the target, called the *cochonnet*. The *cochonnet*, or "piglet," is a smaller, wooden ball. Part of the fun is for players to bump the other team's balls out of the way with their own balls!

(right) A man prepares to throw his boules.

(above) A pétanque player measures the distance between the boules and the cochonnet to see who is the winner.

Rules for *pétanque*

Pétanque is a simple game that you can play with your family or friends. You need:
- at least two players
- a large, flat, open area
- two balls per person, each about the size of a large orange
- a golfball-sized *cochonnet*
- string

1. Place the *cochonnet* on the ground and take ten steps back. Lay a string at that spot to mark the starting line.

2. Organize the players into two equal teams. Each team member gets two balls.

3. A player from the first team stands behind the string and tosses a ball as close as possible to the *cochonnet*. Then, a player from the second team tosses, trying to get the ball even closer to the *cochonnet* or to knock the opponent's ball out of the way. The teams alternate until they throw all their balls.

4. The team whose ball is closest to the *cochonnet* scores one point. That team scores an additional point for each ball that is closer to the target than the other team's.

5. Pick up the balls and continue play. The first team to reach thirteen points wins.

Cooking is an art in France. The French think of dining as one of life's greatest joys. They prefer to linger over their meals rather than eat quickly. The finest French restaurants serve *haute cuisine*, or expensive, elaborate dishes made from the best ingredients. Even ordinary French meals are skillfully prepared and delicious.

A fine tradition

The art of cooking has long been a part of life in France. About 400 years ago, the French queen Marie de Médici hired Italian chefs to prepare fine meals at the royal palace. The food was so delicious that wealthy families all over the country soon hired newly trained French chefs. Ordinary people ate poorly, however, or even went hungry.

The first restaurants

When the French Revolution began, chefs lost their jobs. To earn money, they set up the country's first restaurants, where people could pay to try their fine food. As France prospered in the nineteenth and twentieth centuries, better food became widely available and fine cooking skills spread throughout the country. Today, French chefs are known all over the world. Some have even opened cooking schools in countries such as the United States and Japan.

Alain Ducasse, one of France's most famous chefs, prepares sauces at his restaurant in Paris.

The café experience

For years, people have gone to cafés for a coffee, a meal, to meet friends, or just to watch passers-by on the street. France's cafés were also favorite gathering places for famous artists, writers, and philosophers. Today, cafés remain an important part of social life in small towns. They are not as popular as they once were in big cities, however, where many people now grab snacks from American-style fast-food restaurants.

Food around France

Cooks in each part of France have their own specialties, depending on which ingredients are available locally. In the north, where there are many dairy farms, foods are made with butter and cream. The far south produces olive oil, garlic, and herbs, which are used as main ingredients.

Judges at a cooking competition in Biarritz, in southwestern France, sample many different fish stews to choose the winner.

All kinds of meat are popular in France. Beef, chicken, pork, rabbit, lamb, and various types of **game** are often served with rich sauces. In the northeast, cold cooked meats and sausages are favorite foods. Seafood, including mussels, oysters, lobster, salmon, and herring, is a specialty along the coasts. One famous **delicacy** enjoyed throughout France and the world is *escargots*, which are snails cooked in garlic butter. Diners use special tongs to remove the *escargots* from their shells.

Breads

Fresh-baked breads are a main part of every meal. The most popular type of bread is the long, thin, crusty *baguette*. When eating a *baguette* or any other kind of bread, it is customary to break off chunks rather than slice it.

*The owners of a **boulangerie** proudly show off some of the many types of bread that they bake.*

Sweets

Rich French pastries come in all shapes and sizes. Pastry chefs spend hours decorating them with chopped fruits and nuts, chocolate, and **glazes**. Fruit tarts and pies, as well as cream-filled *éclairs*, are favorite treats. Other French sweets include a baked fruit pudding called a *clafoutis*; *nougat*, a candy made from almonds and honey; and *crêpes*, which are thin, rolled pancakes filled with fruit or whipped cream.

Make a fruity *clafoutis*

Make a *clafoutis* with the help of an adult. You can fill the *clafoutis* with different fruit, depending on the season. This recipe calls for peaches, but try cherries, pears, plums, nectarines, or apricots. You will need:

10 peaches
3 eggs
250 mL (1 cup) milk
75 mL ($\frac{1}{4}$ cup) cream
75 mL ($\frac{1}{4}$ cup) sugar
170 mL ($\frac{2}{3}$ cup) sifted all-purpose flour

15 mL (1 tbsp) vanilla extract
butter or margarine
a dash of salt
a mixing bowl and electric mixer
a large, shallow baking dish

1. Preheat the oven to 175°C (350°F). Grease the baking dish with butter or margarine.

2. Wash and slice the peaches, removing the stones and the skin. Set the peach slices aside.

3. Mix the eggs, milk, cream, sugar, flour, vanilla, and salt in the bowl. Beat with a mixer for about five minutes, until foamy.

4. Pour enough mixture into the baking dish to cover the bottom. Place it in the oven.

5. After 2 to 3 minutes, remove the dish from the oven. Lay the peach slices on the bottom of the dish. Pour the leftover mixture over the peaches.

6. Bake for 30 to 35 minutes, or until the *clafoutis* is puffed and browned. Serve warm, sprinkled with sugar.

A family enjoys a picnic of cheese, vegetables, apples, bread, chicken, and a tart by the Loire River.

Fine French wine

In France, no main course is complete without wine. The country makes a quarter of all the world's wine. Each region produces a different variety, depending on the type of grapes that grow there. The wines can often be distinguished by the shape and color of their bottle.

From vine to wine

Two thousand years ago, the Romans introduced grape growing and the art of winemaking to France. Today, winemakers still use these same basic methods. After months of careful farming, they harvest white and red grapes from the vines and crush them to squeeze out their juice. This juice ferments, which means that its sugars turn into alcohol. Once it ferments, the juice becomes wine.

(right) A grape picker pours a pail of just-harvested grapes into a huge bin.

(bottom) Wine is stored and aged in large barrels in a cellar.

More flavor

A wine's flavor depends on the kind of grapes used and how the juice is treated after it ferments. Many fermented wines are aged in oak barrels before they are bottled. This process gives the wines a fuller, woodlike flavor. To make **champagne**, yeast and sugar are added after the fermented wine is bottled, and then it is left to ferment a second time. When the yeast and sugar mix, they create a gas called carbon dioxide which produces bubbles. The bubbles stay in the bottle and make the champagne fizzy.

Camembert cheese sits on shelves in cheese caves for 21 days until it has ripened and is ready to be eaten.

(above) Visitors to a winery sample the latest batch of wine.

Say cheese and more cheese!

The French leader General Charles de Gaulle once commented on how big a job it was to run his country. He said, "Nobody can simply bring together a country that has over 265 kinds of cheese!" Today, there are over 400 official *fromages*, or cheeses, in France. No other country has as many varieties, and French cheese manufacturers are always trying to invent more. The cheeses are made from fresh local milk, produced by France's large dairy industry.

(below) Different types of Roquefort cheese, each with a slightly different flavor, are displayed in a special cheese store called a **fromager affineur.**

Roquefort Papillon
Carte Noire (lait de brebis)
Rouergue A.O.C
45 % m.g.

le kg   161 fr

Roquefort Carles
(Rouergue)
(lait de brebis) artisanal
A.O.C   45 % m.g.

le kg   161 fr

Shopping

French villages, towns, and cities have many different kinds of stores with a dazzling array of products. Most people prefer to shop at small, local stores, but large supermarkets and department stores are becoming more popular. People usually buy meat, bread, and milk each day. Their daily outings, however, are for more than just stocking up on food! It also gives them the chance to learn the latest gossip from local shopkeepers.

In the neighborhood

Neighborhood stores usually specialize in one kind of product. There is the *crèmerie*, or diary store; the *boulangerie*, or bakery; and the *boucherie*, or butcher's shop. People visit the *patisserie* to buy pastries, chocolates, and other sweets, and the *poissonerie* to buy seafood. Other neighborhood stores include the *pharmacie*, or drug store, and the *maison de la presse*, where customers can purchase newspapers, magazines and books.

*Cold cuts and sausages hang from a **boucherie**, which also sells **paté**, a meat paste for spreading on bread or crackers.*

Food shops line this quaint street in the old part of Saint Rémy, in southeast France.

Many markets

Every town and city has a busy market place, where local farmers and merchants sell their produce and wares. At the market, shoppers can buy everything from eggs and flowers to clothes and household goods. One of Europe's largest flea markets, *Le Marché aux Puces St-Ouen*, has been in Paris for about a hundred years. Filling many alleyways, it is made up of a jumble of stalls selling second-hand clothes, antiques, and jewelry.

Hypermarchés

Hypermarchés, or hypermarkets, are a combination of North American supermarkets and department stores. These giant stores, located in the suburbs, are fairly new to France. Shoppers can find just about any food item at the *hypermarché*, in addition to products such as lawnmowers and clothing.

Fashionable Paris

Paris is known as one of the most exciting places in the world to shop for clothing, perfumes, and gourmet foods. Some of its more glamorous stores are clothing stores, which display the latest styles by French designers. Most people cannot afford the designer fashions, though, so they just window shop.

(above) Skateboarders practise their skills on the steps of a Paris building.

(above) Shoppers buy flowers at a covered outdoor market in Antibes on the Mediterranean Sea.

(below) While walking her dog, a woman window shops to look at Christian Dior, a designer clothing store in Paris.

Marcel tucks his soccer ball tightly under his arm as he runs down the Paris streets to his family's six-story apartment building. He promised that he would not be late for Sunday lunch with his grandparents! After stopping at the corner *boulangerie* for the *baguettes* his father requested, he bolts down the sidewalk and through the door of his building, surprising Monsieur Vergé, the caretaker.

"Slow down!" Monsieur Vergé warns as Marcel runs up the flights of stairs that lead to his apartment. Marcel's father and older sister Marie are setting the table as he bursts in.

"I'm sorry I'm late, Papa," he apologizes, placing the soccer ball by the door. "I lost track of time."

Marcel practices bouncing a soccer ball on his head. If he does not hurry home, he will be late for lunch.

Marcel's friends are spending the afternoon skateboarding. Marcel hopes to catch up with them after lunch.

Marie makes a face at him, but his father just smiles, takes the *baguettes*, and says, "Grand-mère and Grand-père are in the living room with Maman. Get washed and changed. Lunch will be ready in a couple minutes."

As Marcel puts on clean clothes, he glances at his suitcase. It's all packed for his week-long school vacation to the mysterious megaliths, or standing stones, in Carnac, in northwest France.

When Marcel returns to the dining room, everyone is just about ready to sit down at the table. He says hello, hugs his grandparents, and gives them each *bises*, or kisses, on the cheeks. Then, Maman passes around the bread and wine, and the family begins to eat. After some cold-meat appetizers, Papa serves a *bouillabaisse*, a dish of fish and other seafood served in a broth with slices of bread. Lunch ends with a salad, a piece of cheese, and a slice of peach *clafoutis*. Then, everyone relaxes over a cup of fresh coffee.

Soon, Papa and Grand-père turn on the television to check the latest results of the French Open tennis tournament. Marcel helps Maman, Grand-mère, and Marie clear the table. Then, he and Marie check his train's departure time on the *Minitel*, a computer terminal connected to the telephone line. He's leaving tomorrow and doesn't want to miss his trip! After checking the time, Marcel goes to the door and puts on his shoes and jacket.

Chimère strolls across the street after slipping out of the building when Marcel left to meet his friends.

"Are you going out again?" Maman asks. "I have all my stuff packed for the trip tomorrow," Marcel replies. "I thought I would meet my friends at the café for a while and then maybe go skateboarding at the park."

"I suppose," his mother says. "Just don't be too late." "I won't be," Marcel replies. Then, he kisses his grandparents good-bye and, skateboard under his arm, jogs out the door and downstairs to the street.

*Using the **Minitel**, Marie finds out that Marcel's train is scheduled to leave an hour earlier than expected.*

Glossary

Allies The group of countries that fought against Germany, Italy, and Japan during World War II

ancestor A person from whom one is descended

apprentice A person learning a trade by working with someone who is more experienced

architect A designer of buildings

bankrupt Having no money to pay back the money one owes

champagne A bubbly wine made in the region of Champagne, in France, which people often drink for celebrations

claim To demand as one's own

colony An area controlled by a distant country

conquer To gain control over a land using force

custom Something that a group of people has done for so long that it becomes an important part of their way of life

delicacy A fine food

democracy A form of government in which representatives are elected to make decisions for a society

descendant A person who can trace his or her family roots to a certain family or group

emperor A ruler of a country or group of countries

empire A group of countries under one ruler or government

execute To put to death

game Wild animals that are killed for sport or food

glaze A shiny clear icing

homeland An area that is identified with a particular group of people

immigrant A person who settles in another country

industry A business that manufactures or sells a product

invade To enter with force

livestock Farm animals

monument A structure built to remember a person or event

occupied The invasion and control of a country by a foriegn army

philosopher A person who tries to explain the laws of the universe

rebel A person who opposes a government or ruler

reign The period that a ruler is in power

renovation The process of repairing a building so that it is in better condition

republic A country, usually led by a president, in which the citizens elect government representatives

revolution The overthrow of a government

rural Relating to the countryside

shepherdess A girl or woman who takes care of sheep

stake A post to which someone is tied and killed by burning

technical school A school where someone learns a trade

trade A type of work done by hand that requires special skill

troop A group of soldiers

urban Relating to the city

Index

1 2 3 4 5 6 7 8 9 0 Printed in the USA 5 4 3 2 1 0